D1443891

THE 7 CONTINENTS

AFRICA

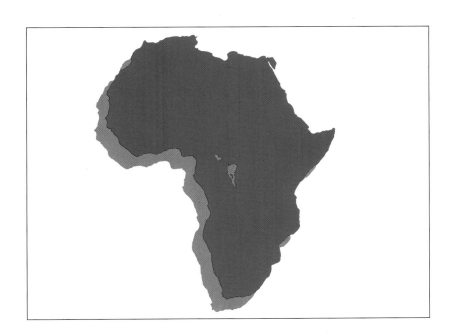

APRIL PULLEY SAYRE

O.W. HOLMES JR. HIGH LIBRARY
1220 Drexel Dr.
Davis, CA 95616

TWENTY-FIRST CENTURY BOOKS
BROOKFIELD, CONNECTICUT

For librarians, who love tackling the big topics and uncovering hidden facts.

Thanks especially to the librarians and other staff of the St. Joseph County Public Library, my local gold mine.

—A.P.S.

Published by Twenty-First Century Books
A Division of The Millbrook Press, Inc.
2 Old New Milford Road
Brookfield, Connecticut 06804

Text copyright © 1999 by April Pulley Sayre
Maps by Joe LeMonnier
All rights reserved.

Library of Congress Cataloging-in-Publication Data
Sayre, April Pulley.
Africa / April Pulley Sayre.
p. cm. — (The seven continents)
Includes bibliographical references and index.
Summary: Describes the countries, landscapes, geology, weather, climate,
air, soil, plants, and animals of the continent of Asia.

ISBN 0-7613-1367-2 (lib. bdg.)
1. Africa—Juvenile literature. [1. Africa.] I. Title.
II. Series: Sayre, April Pulley. 7 continents.
DT22.S3 1999
960—dc21   99-14430
                                                                CIP
                                                                 AC

Printed in the United States of America
1 3 5 4 2

Photo Credits

Cover photograph courtesy of Liaison Agency (© C. & M. Huot)

Photographs courtesy of Photo Researchers, Inc.: pp. 8 (© Len Rue, Jr.), 27 (© George Holton), 30 (© Jacques Jangoux), 35 (top, © Tom McHugh/Steinhart Aquarium), 47 (© Kenneth W. Fink/National Audubon Society), 54 (© James Hancock); Liaison Agency: pp. 15 (© Beziau/Boisberrange), 20 (© Gilles Mingasson), 24 (© Sidali/Djenidi), 39 (© Alexis Georgeon), 40 (© Daniel J. Cox); © Wolfgang Kaehler: pp. 16, 36, 51;Anthro-Photo: p. 28 (© Edward Tronick); Peter Arnold, Inc.: pp. 33 (© Arthus-Bertrand), 34 (© M. & C. Denis-Huot), 35 (bottom, © Diane Blell), 37 (© Fritz Polking), 44 (© H. R. Bramaz), 45 (© Diane Blell); © Dominic Barth: p. 50

CONTENTS

Introduction CONTINENTS: WHERE WE STAND 5

One KEYS TO THE CONTINENT 9

Two NORTHERN AFRICA: SPOTLIGHT ON THE SAHARA 14

Three CENTRAL AND WEST AFRICA 25

Four EASTERN AFRICA: THE GREAT RIFT VALLEY 32

Five SOUTHERN AFRICA 42

Conclusion LOOKING TO THE FUTURE 53

Glossary 56

Political Map of Africa 58

Independent Countries Located in Africa 59

Further Reading 61

Index 63

INTRODUCTION

CONTINENTS: WHERE WE STAND

The ground you stand on may seem solid and stable, but it's really moving all the time. How is that possible? Because all of the earth's continents, islands, oceans, and people ride on tectonic plates. These plates, which are huge slabs of the earth's crust, float on top of hot, melted rock below. One plate may carry a whole continent and a piece of an ocean. Another may carry only a few islands and some ocean. The plates shift, slide, and even bump together slowly as the molten rock below them flows.

Plate edges are where the action is, geologically speaking. That's where volcanoes erupt and earthquakes shake the land. Tectonic plates collide, gradually crumpling continents into folds that become mountains. Dry land, or ocean floor, can be made at these plate edges. Melted rock, spurting out of volcanoes or oozing out of cracks between plates, cools and solidifies. Dry land, or ocean floor, can also be destroyed here, as the edge of one tectonic plate slips underneath another. The moving, grinding plates create tremendous pressure and heat, which melts the rock, turning it into semisolid material.

Continents, the world's largest landmasses, the rock rafts where we live, ride on this shifting puzzle of tectonic plates. These continents are made of material that floated to the surface when much of the earth was hot and liquid long ago. The floating material then cooled and became solid. Two hundred and fifty million years ago there was only one continent, the supercontinent Pangaea, surrounded by one ocean, Panthalassa. But since then, the tectonic plates have moved, breaking apart the continents and rearranging them. Today there are seven continents: North America, South America, Europe, Asia, Africa, Australia, and Antarctica.

250 Million Years Ago

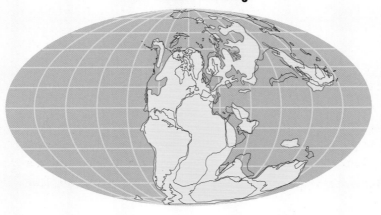

Two hundred and fifty million years ago there was only one continent and one ocean, as shown above. (Rough shapes the continents would eventually take are outlined in black.) The view below shows where the seven continents are today. These positions will continue to change slowly as tectonic plates shift.

Present Day

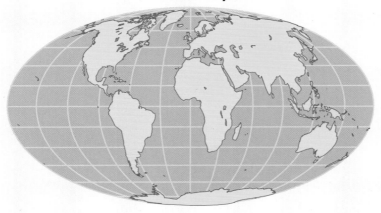

Each continent has its own unique character and conditions, shaped by its history and position on the earth. Europe, which is connected to Asia, has lots of coastline and moist, ocean air. Australia, meanwhile, is influenced by its neighbor, Antarctica, which sends cool currents northward to its shores. North America and South America were once separated, but are now connected by Panama. Over the years, animals, from ancient camels to armadillos, have traveled the bridge in between these two continents.

A continent's landscape, geology, weather, and natural communities affect almost every human action taken on that continent, from planting a seed to waging a war. Rivers become the borders of countries. Soil determines what we can grow. Weather and climate affect our cultures—what we feel, how we dress, even how we celebrate.

Understanding continents can give us a deeper knowledge of the earth—its plants, animals, and people. It can help us see behind news headlines to appreciate the forces that shape world events. Such knowledge can be helpful, especially in a world that's constantly changing and shifting, down to the very earth beneath our feet.

A herd of Burchell's zebra in Kenya. Notice the zebra keeping an eye on the photographer. If it senses danger, this zebra will alert the rest of the herd to move along.

1

KEYS TO THE CONTINENT

If you close your eyes and picture Africa, what do you see in your mind? Giraffes' long necks stretching up to pick tree leaves? Elephants at a waterhole, using their trunks like showerheads? How about zebras, their striped backs flashing as they gallop beneath the tropical sun? Giraffes, elephants, and zebras are among many common zoo animals native to Africa's savannas, dry grasslands with scattered trees.

Savannas and other grasslands cover 40 percent of Africa. They are home to tremendous herds of wildebeest, antelope, giraffe, and zebra. Savannas are also the home of the high-speed chase, in which predators such as cheetahs, lions, and wild dogs chase and kill herd animals. These daily dramas have made African savanna animals a popular topic for nature documentaries. But Africa has other landscapes and other animals that deserve the spotlight, too.

In Africa's rain forests, centered in the Democratic Republic of the Congo, forest elephants wander and pygmy hippos wallow. Lowland gorillas munch on stems as flocks of African gray parrots fly. These forests support a very high species diversity—number of plant and animal types—from beetles to chimpanzees. Scientists are still discovering new insect species here and are just beginning to study many of the large animals in these forests.

To the north, south, and east of Africa's rain forests, rainfall gradually decreases and woodlands grow. Woodlands are a type of forest with very little undergrowth and large trees that grow relatively far apart. Elephants shake these trees to make seedpods fall to the ground. Then they feast on the pods. A patchwork of woodlands, savannas, and steppes—a type of treeless grassland—covers most of Africa's semidry, also called semi-arid, land.

The driest lands, of course, are deserts. And if you like deserts, you'll love Africa. Two-fifths of the continent is desert. Northern Africa is blanketed by the Sahara, Earth's largest desert. Its quiet spaces, curved dunes, and pebbled expanses have a harsh beauty all their own. But lack of water and food makes life difficult for animals, plants, and people in the Sahara.

South of Africa's rain forests are savannas, woodlands, steppes, and two major dry areas: the Kalahari Desert and Namib Desert. The Kalahari and Namib, despite their dryness, support more wildlife than the Sahara and are home to a variety of lizards, birds, and other creatures. (Most scientists would say that the Kalahari, despite its name, is not a desert at all.)

The extreme northern and extreme southern coasts of Africa are slightly cooler and moister than Africa's interior. Just north of the Sahara, along the shores of the Mediterranean Sea, shrubs and crops thrive. Orchards of olive trees and orange trees and fields of tomatoes and eggplants grow here. Fishing boats from the Atlantic Ocean and Mediterranean bring in fish, which are used in the colorful, spicy, native cuisine.

Africa, from its moist forests to its dry deserts, from its icy mountaintops to its steamy swamps, supports a spectacular variety of animals and plants. It is the best place on Earth to see tremendous herds of large animals. In many ways, it *is* the wildlife continent.

AFRICA: THE LAY OF THE LAND

Africa is the second-largest continent on Earth stretching 4,737 miles (7,623 kilometers) from north to south and 4,511 miles (7,260 kilometers) from east to west. It is surrounded by the Red Sea, the Indian Ocean, the Atlantic Ocean, and the Mediterranean Sea. To the east it was once connected to Asia by the Isthmus of Suez, but the digging of the Suez Canal divided the two continents.

Politically, Africa is complex; it contains fifty-three countries, more than any other continent. It has many islands offshore, including the Canary Islands and Madagascar, the fourth-largest island in the world.

Mainland Africa is made up mostly of plateaus: relatively flat, raised areas of land. In between these plateaus are basins: large, bowl-shaped regions such as the Kalahari Basin of southern Africa and the Congo Basin, where the Democratic Republic of the Congo's rain forests are located. Africa's three major mountain regions are the Atlas Mountains of northern Africa, the Drakensberg Mountains of South Africa, and the mountains of the Great Rift Valley. Smaller, more isolated mountains exist elsewhere in Africa—even in the middle of the Sahara Desert.

Africa's Great Rift Valley is a series of immense, parallel cracks in the earth. The Great Rift Valley extends from the Red Sea through East Africa to Mozambique. The string of lakes that fill its valleys makes it easy to identify the Great Rift on a map.

Volcanoes and earthquakes occur along the Great Rift Valley, but compared to Asia, Europe, and North America, Africa is a geologically old and quiet land. It experiences far fewer earthquakes and volcanic eruptions than South America. Africa, except on its coldest mountaintops, also has not been shaped by glaciation—the movement of glaciers during the earth's last Ice Age. Eleven thousand years ago, these glaciers drastically changed the landscape in Europe, Asia, and North America, creating lakes and scraping soil off the land. But Africa's ancient soils and rock layers remained virtually unchanged.

Because Africa has been largely unchanged by glaciation, and because much of the land is desert and bare of plants, the continent is an ideal place for scientists to dig down into rock layers to study animals and people of long ago. In Egypt's El Faiyum region, scientists sweep away sand with brooms to find the bones of primates that lived a million years ago. In Olduvai Gorge in East Africa, anthropologists have found fossilized human footprints 3.6 million years old!

WORLD RECORDS HELD BY AFRICA

- Second-largest continent (Asia is the largest)
- Longest river: Nile, about 4,160 miles (6,693 kilometers) in length
- Largest desert: Sahara, 3.5 million square miles (9,065,000 square kilometers)
- Hottest shade temperature: 136°F (58°C), Al'Aziziyah, Libya, September 13, 1922
- Second-deepest lake: Lake Tanganyika, between Tanzania and The Democratic Republic of the Congo, 4,710 feet (1,436 meters) deep

STATISTICS AND RECORDS FOR THE CONTINENT OF AFRICA

- Area: 11,700,000 square miles (30,300,000 square kilometers)—about 20 percent of the earth's land.
- Population: estimated 763,000,000
- Largest lake: Lake Victoria, shared by Uganda, Kenya, and Tanzania, 25,560 square miles (68,880 square kilometers)
- Highest point: Mt. Kilimanjaro, Tanzania, 19,340 feet (5,895 meters)
- Lowest Point: Lake Assal, Djibouti, 512 feet (156 meters) below sea level

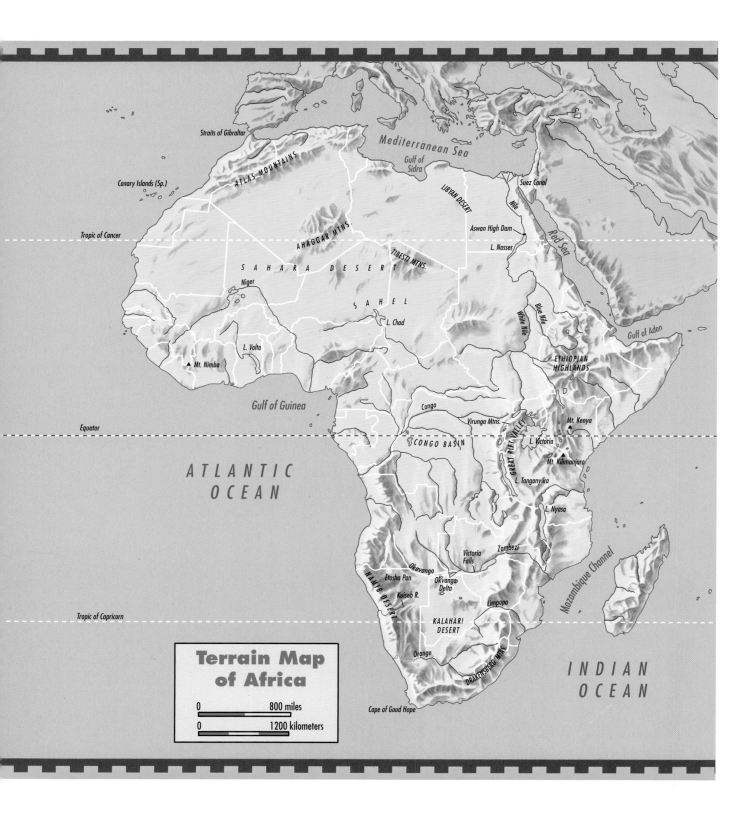

Terrain Map of Africa

0 — 800 miles
0 — 1200 kilometers

Straits of Gibraltar

Mediterranean Sea

Gulf of Sidra

Canary Islands (Sp.)

ATLAS MOUNTAINS

LIBYAN DESERT

Suez Canal

Nile

Tropic of Cancer

AHAGGAR MTNS.

Aswan High Dam

L. Nasser

Red Sea

SAHARA DESERT

TIBESTI MTNS.

Niger

SAHEL

L. Chad

White Nile

Blue Nile

Gulf of Aden

L. Volta

ETHIOPIAN HIGHLANDS

Mt. Nimba

Gulf of Guinea

Congo

Virunga Mtns.

Mt. Kenya

Equator

CONGO BASIN

GREAT RIFT VALLEY

L. Victoria

Mt. Kilimanjaro

ATLANTIC OCEAN

L. Tanganyika

L. Nyasa

Victoria Falls

Zambezi

Okavango

Etosha Pan

Okvango Delta

NAMIB DESERT

Kuiseb R.

Limpopo

Mozambique Channel

Tropic of Capricorn

KALAHARI DESERT

INDIAN OCEAN

Orange

DRAKENSBERG MTNS.

Cape of Good Hope

AFRICA'S FIVE REGIONS

When people discuss Africa, they talk about five major regions: northern, western, central, eastern, and southern. Familiarize yourself with these regions and you'll be in the know for most discussions of Africa. Below are the locations and countries included in each region. (People may disagree on the exact listing of countries in each region.)

Northern Africa encompasses the Sahara Desert and stretches from the Atlantic Coast to the Red Sea. Countries: Algeria, Chad, Egypt, Libya, Mali, Mauritania, Morocco, Niger, Sudan, Tunisia, Western Sahara

Western Africa includes the many countries clustered around the western curve of the continent, adjacent to the Gulf of Guinea and the Atlantic Ocean. Countries: Benin, Burkina Faso, Côte d'Ivoire, Gambia, Ghana, Guinea, Guinea-Bisseau, Liberia, Nigeria, Senegal, Sierra Leone, Togo

Central Africa describes the countries to the west of the Great Rift Valley of Africa, located just north of southern Africa. Countries: Angola, Cameroon, Central African Republic, Congo, Equatorial Guinea, Gabon, The Democratic Republic of the Congo, Zambia

Eastern Africa commonly called East Africa, describes countries between northern Africa and southern Africa and east of the Great Rift. Countries: Burundi, Djibouti, Ethiopia, Kenya, Rwanda, Somalia, Tanzania, Uganda.

Southern Africa consists of countries at the southern tip of the continent, plus the nearby island of Madagascar. Countries: Botswana, Lesotho, Madagascar, Malawi, Mozambique, Namibia, Swaziland, South Africa, Zimbabwe

2

NORTHERN AFRICA: SPOTLIGHT ON THE SAHARA

The Sahara Desert, the largest desert on Earth, dominates northern Africa. Covering 3.5 million square miles (9,065,000 square kilometers), this immense desert is nearly as big as the United States! Northern Africa, however, isn't all desert. In the east is the Nile Valley, where river water makes agriculture possible. Just north of the Sahara lies a thin sliver of coastal land where the climate is slightly wetter and cooler. Bushes, small trees, and spring wildflowers create a pleasant Mediterranean scene. The snow-capped Atlas Mountains, jutting up near the Moroccan coast, vary the landscape even more. Just south of the Sahara lies the Sahel, a transitional area that is not as dry as the Sahara. This region, made up of semidesert, with grasslands and dry woodlands, stretches from Mauritania to Chad.

WELCOME TO THE SAHARA

If you plan to explore the Sahara, be prepared for heat, for sun, for wind, for dryness, and oddly enough, for cold. During the daytime you may swelter in temperatures of more than 110°F (43°C). The hottest air temperature ever recorded on Earth was in the Sahara, at Al'Aziziyah, Libya, when it was a chocolate-melting 136°F (58°C) in the shade! Yet at night, the desert cools off quickly. After sunset, the temperature can drop as much as 100°F (37.8°C), leaving you shivering even in a sleeping bag.

The reason the desert cools so much at night is that the air is very dry. Deserts do not have a blanket of humid air to slow down the escape of heat into space after nightfall.

14

A desolate scene in the Tadrart Mountains of southwestern Libya. There are ancient drawings and engravings in the mountains' caves.

Moister climates, such as rain forests, are insulated by such a layer of humid air. Trees and other plants slowly release water through their leaves to the air through a process called transpiration. This water evaporates from the leaves into the air. Water vapor in the air heats up and cools off slowly, moderating temperatures. The Sahara Desert also lacks the trees, bushes, and grasses that blanket other biomes and help insulate them.

DEADLY DRYNESS

Dryness, or aridity, is a fact of life in the Sahara. Each year the Sahara Desert receives less than 4 inches (10 centimeters) of rain on average. Parts of the Sahara can go without rain for several years! Intense sunlight and a hot climate make water evaporate quickly. Strong winds, which can blow at speeds of 62 miles (100 kilometers) per hour make things dry out even faster. To prevent water loss, Saharan plants have small leaves and waxy leaf surfaces. Out in the Sahara, people's bodies, which are about two-thirds water, are at risk. Mild dehydration—the loss of water—may cause dry, cracked lips, or thirst. Severely dehydrated people can become delirious, suffer kidney failure, and even die.

SAHARA'S SANDPAPER WINDS

What can rub your skin raw, clog up a truck's engine, and scour the paint off a car? A sandstorm. Hot Saharan winds carry sand and dust up into the air, creating sand and dust storms. During a sandstorm it is hard to keep sand and grit out of your eyes, and it can be very difficult to see. The cloth headdresses of many desert people not only keep the sun off them, but can be wrapped around the face to keep out choking sand and dust. Like sandpaper, the sandy wind can even rub skin raw. The sand-laden winds can sandblast windshields, making thousands of tiny pit marks, until car windows look frosty and are impossible to see through. Sand can also cover roads and cars, completely burying them.

A dust storm darkens the sky in Mali, near Timbuktu. The Tuareg people shown here are nomadic, and they will soon move on to their next camp.

16

ERGS, HAMMADAS, AND CHOTTS

When most people picture the Sahara, they imagine sand dunes stretching as far as the eye can see. These seas of sand, called ergs, do cover about 20 percent of the Sahara. Saharan dunes can be 1,000 feet (300 meters) tall and stretch for 600 miles (1,000 kilometers)! Wind sculpts the dunes, constantly changing both their shape and position.

Even more of the Sahara, about 70 percent, is made up of stony deserts known as regs. Regs are relatively flat and covered by small gravel. The sand has been carried away by wind. Rocks that remain develop a dark sheen, called desert varnish, caused by chemicals in the wind and rain. In parts of the Sahara, the ground is covered with salt left over from dried up lakes. These salt flats, called chotts, are sometimes mined for salt.

Ergs, regs, and chotts are not all you can see in the Sahara. This desert has its high points: mountains and hammadas, which are plateaus. The two-million-year-old Ahaggar Mountains in southern Algeria and Libya tower 9,852 feet (3,000 meters) above the central Sahara, and Emi Koussi, in the Tibesti Mountains, is 11,204 feet (3,415 meters) high.

TURN LEFT AT THE MILLIONTH PEBBLE

Getting lost in the Sahara is easy. Mountains, dunes, and hammadas are some of the only noticeable landscape features. In places, there aren't any trees, boulders, or other landmarks to help judge direction or distance. Roads can quickly be covered by blowing sand. You can walk over dune after dune and end up going in a circle, especially if the dunes are curved. What makes matters worse is that heated air rising up off the hot ground can make things look blurry at a distance. What you think is a lake may turn out to be a mirage.

OH, FOR AN OASIS!

Getting lost is not the only desert danger. Dying of thirst is a real possibility. Wadis, the dry channels of desert rivers, only fill with water after rain. Rain, of course, is scarce in such a dry climate. So, for thousands of years travelers have relied on oases, small desert areas where water bubbles out of the ground from natural springs. These oases provide food and water for travelers and their animals. Saharan oases also support palm trees, irrigated fields, and small villages.

Oasis water comes from aquifers, porous underground layers of sandstone. Rain that has fallen over thousands of years, or in wetter regions, flows through spaces between the rocks in these layers. Where the rock layers have been folded or eroded by wind or water, part of a layer may be exposed at the ground's surface, creating an oasis. In recent years, people have installed wells with pumps to bring up more water from aquifers for household use and for watering crops. Unfortunately, water is being used faster than it is being replaced by the Sahara's infrequent rains. In places, aquifer water levels are dropping out of reach of tree roots, causing trees to die. Some natural oases have dried up entirely.

17

NEED A DATE?

Dates, a sweet fruit used in cookies and breads by North Americans, are eaten much more widely in Africa. Dates grow on date palms, trees that are native to the Arabian Peninsula but are also planted all over northern Africa. Date palm plantations cover hundreds of thousands of acres of Morocco. The trees look like the coconut palms of the Caribbean islands, but instead of coconuts, the date palms produce huge clusters of date fruits. There are more than a hundred different date varieties, in different sizes and colors. The date palm not only produces fruit, but is also a source of wood. In addition, its leaves are woven to make baskets or mats.

DESERT ANIMALS BEAT THE HEAT

Animals, like plants, are scarce in the Sahara. During the day you might see a spider, a beetle, or an agama lizard scampering over rocks or dunes. But most other animals are inactive, at least part of the day, to stay cool. Birds such as mourning wheatears, desert sparrows, and hoopoe larks take shelter under shady bushes during the heat of the day. Fennec foxes, elephant shrews, and monitor lizards hide out in cool, underground burrows. Scorpions and snakes called horned vipers take shelter under rocks, crawling out when night falls.

After sunset, these nocturnal, or night-active, animals emerge to search for food. Fennec foxes hunt jerboas, small, mouse-sized rodents that hop like kangaroos, on very long hind legs. Desert eagle owls use their acute hearing and sharp eyesight to search for lizards and snakes.

NILE: GREEN RIBBON OF LIFE

Running through the dry, barren Sahara is a ribbon of life: the Nile River. The Nile flows northward from Lake Victoria to the Mediterranean Sea. For seven thousand years the people of Egypt have farmed land along the Nile. Yearly floods would submerge the riverside fields, depositing thick, rich sediment that was good for farming. As the river water receded, the farmers planted their crops in the fertile soil. Later irrigation pipes and canals were built that also brought water out to the croplands. A broad fertile delta formed where the river water slowed down and dropped its load of sediment in the Mediterranean Sea.

A SINKING FEELING IN CAIRO

In the 1960s the Aswan High Dam was built on the Nile. The dam changed the river's flow. The dam harnesses the power of the flowing water to turn the dam's turbines and produce electricity. But the Aswan High Dam prevents the yearly floods. It holds back 98 percent of the river's sediment. Without sediment from yearly floods, riverside fields have become less fertile. Farmers now must use more and more fertilizers to get crops to grow. Starved of sediment, the delta is shrinking, and sinking, as the sea erodes it. In addition, salty Mediterranean water is pushing inland, destroying the fertility of delta soils.

Egypt's population is increasing rapidly, and the Nile River is showing the strain. Nile water, flowing through canals and irrigation pipes throughout the delta, is filthy, full of human sewage and disease-causing organisms. Much of Egypt's population does not have access to clean water, so diseases can spread easily.

MEDITERRANEAN AND MILD

North of the Sahara, along the Mediterranean coast from Morocco to Egypt, the climate is dry and warm in summer and cooler and wetter in winter. Morocco is just 9 miles (15 kilometers) south of Spain, so it's not surprising that the Moroccan coast has a lot in common with the southern coast of Europe. Both Spain and Morocco have a Mediterranean climate, as does southern California.

From Morocco to Tunisia, the land supports shrubs that are evergreen, which means they are green year round, losing only a few leaves at a time. Trees are stunted and slow growing. After spring rains, blue and gold wildflowers bloom. Many of the same kinds of crops that grow in Spain, Greece, or southern California also grow in northern Africa. Cork oaks, from which the bark is harvested for cork, are common. Marketplaces are full of locally grown tomatoes, olives, oranges, apples, and a wide variety of vegetables. Fishing offshore in the Mediterranean Sea is good, too. For many centuries, the cities along this coast have been busy, colorful ports, as ships have come and gone, exchanging goods between Europe, Africa, and Asia through the Mediterranean Sea. Most of northern Africa's people live in the Mediterranean region, where the climate is pleasant and the soil is fertile.

A "PEAK" AT MOROCCO'S MOUNTAINS

At high altitudes, the air temperature is cooler than in the lowlands. Snow covers the peaks of many of Morocco's Atlas Mountains. The Atlas Mountains are part of the same mountain system as the European Alps. Golden eagles and gray-backed vultures called lammergeiers soar overhead. There is no snow at lower altitudes, and low-growing plants survive. Just a hike downhill are cedar forests, with cedar trees as old as four hundred years. Birds such as firecrests, red crossbills, scops owls, and pied Numidian woodpeckers inhabit these forests, along with Barbary macaques, a type of monkey. At slightly lower altitudes are forests of Argan trees, where Barbary squirrels live. At the base of the Atlas Mountains, steppe grows. Steppe is a dry type of grassland with alfa-grass, jujube bushes, and sagebrush. It is inhabited by animals such as golden jackals and geckos.

19

A Berber home in the Atlas Mountains, in Morocco. The mountains rise in a series of ranges from the Atlantic Ocean to the highest peak, Toubkal, 13,674 feet (4,167 meters) tall.

WELCOME FEATHERED FRIENDS

Africa is not just a destination for people who want to go on safaris. An estimated five billion birds travel from Asia and Europe to Africa in the fall. For some birds, this journey, called migration, can be arduous. For example, white storks fly a remarkable 6,500 miles (10,500 kilometers) from northern Europe to South Africa!

Migrating birds tend to skirt coasts and cross over water wherever the distance is shortest. Along certain travel routes, the sky can fill up with thousands of soaring hawks, circling storks, and songbirds. It's practically an aerial traffic jam! On their way to and from Africa, migrating birds funnel past four major spots: Tangier, Morocco; Cap Bon, Tunisia; the Sinai of Egypt; and the Ras Siyan peninsula, Djibouti. Millions of shorebirds, such as godwits, dunlins, and sandpipers, spend time feeding at the mudflats of Banc D'Arguin National Park in Mauritania. Near Tangier, Morocco, hawks and storks circle over the land before crossing the Mediterranean to Spain during the spring. Wet places such as mudflats along the Nile, coastal mangrove swamps, and desert oases are very important to the survival of these birds. Just about any wet place in northern Africa is a good place to see birds during migration.

PRECARIOUS LIFE IN DRY LANDS

South of the Sahara is the Sahel, a semidesert that receives 10 to 25 inches (25 to 63 centimeters) of rain per year. It supports grasses, bushes, and forests called woodlands. With care, the land can be useful for farming and grazing animals. But the Sahel can only support a small number of people, grazing animals, and farms because water is scarce. Women and children often have to walk several miles each day to reach a spring and collect water to take home for drinking, cooking, and washing.

Dry soils such as the Sahel's are easily damaged. When goats and cattle graze, they not only eat plants, they trample seedlings, and their hooves churn up the soil. Without plants to help hold soil in place, the soil can dry out and blow away. Or it may wash away during heavy rains. This also occurs when people cut down trees and shrubs for fuel wood, leaving the soil unprotected. Either way, what is left behind is barren land unsuitable for growing crops. It may even look like a desert. This kind of damaged land is said to be "desertified."

Despite fragile soils, people have lived in semiarid regions such as the Sahel for thousands of years. Generally, they have lived as nomads, moving from place to place. Shifting herds from one area to another allows plants time to grow and recover after grazing. Limited farming in semidesert areas is possible, too. But farmers must shift their crops, letting some fields lie fallow—unplanted—for a season or more. During fallow periods, the soil can recover some of its fertility. But droughts—long periods without rain—make it impossible to farm these lands in some years.

21

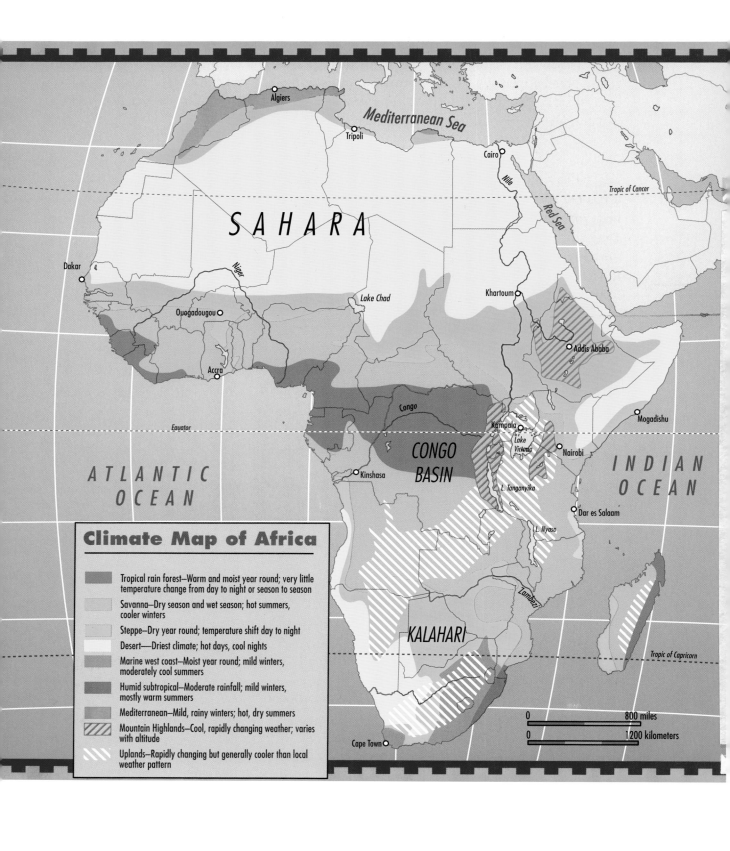

Algiers

Mediterranean Sea

Tripoli

Cairo

Nile

Tropic of Cancer

S A H A R A

Red Sea

Dakar

Niger

Lake Chad

Khartoum

Ouagadougou

Addis Ababa

Accra

Congo

Mogadishu

Equator

CONGO
BASIN

Kampala

Lake Victoria

Nairobi

ATLANTIC
OCEAN

Kinshasa

L. Tanganyika

INDIAN
OCEAN

Dar es Salaam

L. Nyasa

Climate Map of Africa

KALAHARI

Zambezi

- Tropical rain forest—Warm and moist year round; very little temperature change from day to night or season to season
- Savanna—Dry season and wet season; hot summers, cooler winters
- Steppe—Dry year round; temperature shift day to night
- Desert—Driest climate; hot days, cool nights
- Marine west coast—Moist year round; mild winters, moderately cool summers
- Humid subtropical—Moderate rainfall; mild winters, mostly warm summers
- Mediterranean—Mild, rainy winters; hot, dry summers
- Mountain Highlands—Cool, rapidly changing weather; varies with altitude
- Uplands—Rapidly changing but generally cooler than local weather pattern

Tropic of Capricorn

Cape Town

0   800 miles
0   1200 kilometers

Irrigation greatly increases crop yields. But irrigation uses scarce water that may be needed elsewhere. Over time, it can damage the soil by making it too salty for crops to grow. This happens because irrigation water evaporates from the soil, leaving behind natural salts. Year after year, as the water evaporates, the salt builds up in higher and higher concentrations until few, if any, crops grow.

THE DEATH OF PRODUCTIVE LAND: DESERTIFICATION

Desertification, the deterioration of dry lands because of overfarming, overgrazing, improper irrigation, and removal of trees and shrubs, is a major problem in Africa. To help solve this problem, the United Nations has adopted the Convention to Combat Desertification, a treaty that will help countries work together to prevent desertification not only in Africa but also around the world. In some cases, governments will be working to change irrigation systems. They may help farmers buy equipment to farm the soil in ways that make it less vulnerable to erosion. Hopefully these and other efforts will help fight desertification.

DROUGHT AND FAMINE

Droughts can be disastrous for people in semiarid areas such as the Sahel. Crops die. Cattle die without enough grass to eat or water to drink. Famine, an extreme shortage of food, occurs, and people go hungry. People die of thirst, hunger, and disease. Desertification often worsens, as plants die, soil dries out, and land is overgrazed by cattle searching for food. This makes it difficult for the land and people to recover even after the drought ends.

Lately, the global climate seems to be changing, causing more droughts in parts of Africa. This may be part of a natural climate cycle, or it may be linked to air pollution by people. Scientists are still studying the complex connections between climate, drought, desertification, and famine, in hopes of alleviating these problems.

LOOK, IT'S RAINING THE SAHARA!

If you're walking down a street in Florida, a tiny piece of the Sahara might fall on your head. The Sahara is so dusty and windy that some of its dust gets carried high into the atmosphere. Its reddish dust can be carried from the Sahara to Europe and land on rooftops in Spain. Dust can travel west across the Atlantic Ocean to Florida, where it colors the rain slightly pink.

Saharan dust may even affect the growth of coral reefs in the Caribbean Sea. Recently, scientists have discovered that aspergillis, a kind of soil fungus, is killing large patches of Caribbean coral reefs. These scientists suspect the fungus is coming from eroded soil from the Sahara Desert. Years when the fungus has been detected in large amounts in the coral reefs are the same years that the Sahara Desert was experiencing

Desertification. In Southern Algeria, this land has been reduced to sand. There are national and international programs to fight desertification, but there is no substitute for using the land properly.

droughts and lots of Saharan soil was being carried away by winds. More study still needs to be done to confirm this connection between Saharan dust and dying coral reefs in the Caribbean.

But Saharan dust has its good side, too. Scientists from the University of Virginia have discovered that Saharan dust helps fertilize the Amazon rain forest. After the dust travels 3,500 miles (5,600 kilometers) from the Sahara to the Amazon region, heavy rains wash as much as 465,000 tons of dust out of the sky and onto the forest. The Sahara soil contributes phosphate, a chemical compound that helps the forest grow, to the Amazon. The dust-rain forest connection is further evidence that Africa's environment is linked with the environmental health of other continents.

3

CENTRAL AND WEST AFRICA

Sitting very quietly in a rain forest in central Africa, you might see a gorilla chewing stems. A leopard might pad quietly past, and a golden cat might jump from branch to branch above your head. You probably won't remain quiet, however, at least not for long. It's hard to be still when biting ants crawl up your pants, when bees and mosquitoes buzz around your face, or when you spot a leech on your shoe. Africa's rain forests are full of an astounding array of creatures, eating and being eaten.

GREENEST AFRICA: TROPICAL RAIN FOREST

Tropical rain forests only exist in the tropics, the area closest to the equator. In Africa, the equator runs through the Democratic Republic of the Congo, which contains Africa's largest tropical rain forest. This forest, Earth's second largest, extends into Gabon, Congo, and the Central African Republic. Smaller tropical rain forests also occur here and there from Angola through western Africa, and on the islands of Madagascar, Mauritius, Réunion, Rodriguez, and Seychelles. Montane forests, a type of tropical rain forest similar to the cloud forests of South America, also grow on mountains in the Virunga volcano range, bordering The Democratic Republic of the Congo, Rwanda, and Uganda.

WHERE VINES TWINE: FOREST CHARACTERISTICS

Africa's tropical rain forests have many characteristics in common with tropical rain forests elsewhere. Lots of its trees, for instance, have buttresses—skirtlike folds that

25

stretch from the ground up the sides of their trunks. The trees are mostly evergreen, meaning they lose their leaves a few at a time rather than all at once in a season, as deciduous trees do. African rain forest tree leaves also tend to have stiff, broad surfaces, and drip tips, which help drain the rain off leaves. Vines wrap around the trees and twine together in the African forest, as they do in the rain forests of South America.

THE LAYERED LOOK

With tall trees and vines, a tropical rain forest provides many different habitats for animals. Each forest layer has different living conditions, and animals that adapt best to those conditions. The tallest rain forest trees, called emergents, stand out above the rest of the forest. Crowned eagles perch on these trees, where they can get the best "bird's-eye view" of the forest below. The eagles circle, then dive down to catch monkeys, which leap among the treetops in the forest canopy, the next forest layer below.

The canopy is formed from the crowns of the second-tallest rain forest trees. In the canopy, where sunlight is plentiful, leaves, flowers, and fruits are abundant. So are animals. African gray parrots chatter. Monkeys called mandrills climb along tree branches and vines. African giant swallowtails, a type of butterfly, flutter through the treetops. Birds called yellow-casqued hornbills crack open large, colorful fruits. Delicate orchids cling to trees. The entire place is abuzz with bees and other insects flying flower to flower, among the African rubber, okoumé, kapok, and frankincense trees.

Lower down is the understory, where golden cats climb tree trunks and hunt four-striped squirrels. In the dappled shade, chimpanzees snooze in tree forks, and snakes called mambas twine around branches. Down below is the forest floor, where leopards roam and giant snails slowly eat leaves. Chameleons perch quietly on small twigs. Goliath frogs hop. Antelope run through the open spaces between trees. The lowest layer, the forest floor, is quite dark. The trees above block most of the light. The forest floor is warm and humid, so it feels steamy year round.

CONTINENTAL COMPARISONS

Walking into a rain forest in Africa or South America, you would see animals that eat fruit and animals that eat insects. But the animals that fill these roles would be different on each continent. An animal's role, and the part of the environment where it lives, is called its niche. In South America, the animals that eat ants are anteaters. In Africa, giant pangolins, scale-covered creatures, fill that niche. South America has large, fruit-eating birds called toucans. In Africa, hornbills live in a similar way, flying among treetops eating fruit. Although they live on different continents, toucans and hornbills look a lot alike; they have big beaks that are helpful for cracking large nuts and eating fruit. In South America's forests, the niche of big forest floor predator is filled by jaguars. The corresponding niche in Africa is filled by leopards. Both are large, meat-eating cats.

26

Similarities are common among species that inhabit similar niches even if they are continents apart.

Unbelievable Understory Ungulates

One major difference between Africa's and South America's tropical rain forests are the forest floor herbivores. (Herbivores are animals that eat plants.) In South America, large rodents such as pacas and agoutis munch on leaves and fallen fruit. In Africa, however, the forest floor is filled with large ungulates—hoofed animals. Africa's tropical rain forests are home to antelopes such as bongos and duikers. Okapis, a close relative of giraffes, also live there. Standing about 6 feet (1.8 meters) tall, an okapi has chocolate brown fur, a long neck, a head like a horse's, and legs striped like a zebra's. Although local people knew of the okapi, European scientists did not know about this strange-looking animal until about a century ago. A smaller forest ungulate, the chevrotain, has a stomach like a cow's, a body like a deer's, and a head that looks like a chipmunk's. Slender and dainty, chevrotains grow only 16 inches (40 centimeters) tall!

Okapis have very long tongues to strip leaves from trees; they can even clean their ears with their own tongues! This okapi lives along the Ituri River in the Democratic Republic of the Congo.

Scientists are not certain why African rain forests support so many ungulates. But grassy clearings, where these animals can graze in the midst of the forest, seem important to their survival. Elephants, which live in African rain forests, are partially responsible for creating grassy clearings. Elephants pull down branches and chew bark off trees, killing the trees. The trees eventually fall, leaving cleared areas where grass can grow.

How to Hide an Elephant

How do you hide a 7,000-pound (3,200-kilogram) elephant? Put it in a tremendous rain forest. Africa's forest elephants, which are smaller than savanna elephants, are elusive in their rain forest home. It is hard to see the elephants because of the trees. Husband-and-wife research team Richard and Karen Barnes have found that the best way to count the forest elephants accurately is to count elephant droppings. Elephants produce about seventeen droppings per day. The scientists can count fresh droppings in a certain area, then divide by seventeen and come up with an estimate of the number of elephants feeding in that part of the forest. By multiplying this number by the overall area of the forest, they can estimate the number of elephants in the total area.

HONEY HUNTERS

Insects—bees, beetles, ants, praying mantises, and flies—are plentiful in tropical rain forests. In African rain forests, native people such as the Efé take advantage of this abundance. The Efé and many other native peoples eat grubs, the larva of insects. They also climb trees to reach bee nests, using smoke to calm the bees while stealing the honey. The Efé hunt antelope, monkeys, elephants, and other forest animals. Every few weeks, the Efé move their camps to new areas to hunt more game. They trade the meat of wild animals, called bushmeat, to the Lese people, a native group that farms on the edge of the forest. The Lese, in return, give the Efé vegetables and other products. Although the Efé hunt forest animals, scientists believe they have had little impact on the overall animal populations of the forest because the Efé are so small in number.

These Efé children live in the rain forest. Although much of their life is different from yours, laughter is the same around the world.

28

ANIMAL ABUSE: BUSHMEAT AND THE PET TRADE

The meat of wild animals, called bushmeat, is commonly eaten in central and western Africa. People hunt and eat monkeys, parrots, fish eagles, crocodiles, porcupines, antelope, elephants, and just about anything else edible. Market stalls are also filled with foods such as roasted caterpillars, termite larvae, and giant African land snails.

Although laws exist to protect some of the animals, these laws are routinely broken. When people are hungry, they turn to forest animals for meat. And more and more, bushmeat has become a business as rural people sell the animals in exchange for products from cities.

The pet trade, too, has become widespread. African gray parrots, Senegal parrots, and other birds are captured and shipped to Europe and the United States to be sold as pets. For every bird that makes it to the pet store alive, about ten others die during capture or transport. Chimpanzee mothers are killed and eaten; then their babies are sold for pets. You can buy a smoked monkey for only $5, or a baby chimpanzee for $20. The baby chimpanzees, traumatized from being captured and seeing their mothers killed, often die, or if they survive, grow up to be unmanageable, often destructive adults. Trade in animal parts is brisk, too. Gorilla hands and other animal parts are sold in markets for their reputed magical or medicinal properties

Hunting animals by the small number of people native to the forests has never been much of a problem. But the human population has grown rapidly in western and central Africa; as the population has increased, so has the demand for meat. Hunters travel along logging roads and spread out into the forest to kill game. In parts of western Africa, researchers have found that although logging is the greatest threat to wildlife, the bushmeat business is clearly pushing some species toward extinction.

WESTERN AFRICA: GREEN, GOLD, AND GORILLAS

The countries of western Africa, from Sierra Leone to Nigeria, curve around the Gulf of Guinea. To the north, these countries are generally dry and hot, with savannas, land with sparse trees and shrubs. (Some form part of the Sahel.) To the south, the land is greener and moister. Conakry, the capitol of Guinea, receives a skin-soaking 165 inches (4,125 millimeters) of rain each year! Cool currents offshore make coastal regions a little cooler than inland. High temperatures on the coast average only 80°F to 90°F (27°C to 32°C).

Centuries ago, green forests—tropical rain forests and other tropical forest types—stretched across almost all of this region bordering the Gulf of Guinea and the Atlantic. But in the 1880s, logging companies began cutting down the forests. Because of this deforestation—removal of trees—less than 10 percent of the original forest remains in most West African countries today. Areas that were formerly forest are now savanna, palm plantations, pasture, or fields of peanuts, rice, cotton, or cassava. Illegal logging and illegal grazing threatens the remaining forest. National parks have been established in Ghana, Côte D'Ivoire, and Nigeria to protect the forest that is left.

WILDLIFE AND WILD PLACES OF WESTERN AFRICA

Although much of it has been deforested, western Africa is not barren, lifeless land. It contains a wide variety of landscapes and wildlife. The coast of Benin is sandy, with lagoons and marshes full of birds. Inland, the Atakora Mountains contain deep gorges, cliffs, and dramatic scenery. In the far north, where the Niger River bends in a w-shape, is a park shared by Benin, Niger, and Burkina Faso. The W park, named for the river's bend, protects a type of savanna found only in West Africa. It also protects forest, grassland, marsh, and river habitats, where hippos wade, lions roar, cheetahs hunt, crocodiles swim, and ungulates such as duikers, red-fronted gazelles, bushbucks, and hartebeests graze.

Rain forest in Tai National Park, Côte d'Ivoire. Can you imagine making your way through this dense brush, monkeys hooting and birds calling above you?

The country of Gambia, a finger-shaped land almost entirely surrounded by Senegal, contains the Gambia River and riverside land. Although the countryside is mostly planted with peanuts and rice, the riparian, or riverside habitat, includes mudflats and mangrove swamps. Baboons, hippos, and birds such as yellow-billed storks can be seen along the river edge. The Gambia River mouth is home to the endangered West African manatee, a 1,000-pound (450-kilogram) plant-eating mammal. But these animals are rarely seen.

The Côte D'Ivoire's Tai National Park contains the best preserved lowland rain forest in western Africa. Pygmy hippopotamuses swim in its wet areas. Primates such as collared mangabeys, chimpanzees, and colobus monkeys climb through its forests. Birds and butterflies are plentiful. Pangolins, African golden cats, and six species of duikers live in its forests. More than half of the 1,300 plant species in the park are not found anywhere else on Earth.

In addition to savannas, mangrove swamps, tropical rain forests and other forest types, western Africa has biomes that exist only in its mountains. Mount Nimba in the Côte d'Ivoire, has high-altitude grasslands and mist forests—forests with mossy-covered trees kept wet by persistent mist. On top of this mountain is a truly unusual toad called the viviparous toad. It gives birth to baby toads, instead of laying eggs that develop into tadpoles, as other toads do.

A Little Bit of Africa

Somewhere in your house or apartment there is probably a little piece of the African continent. Minerals and oil from Africa are used to manufacture a variety of products, from electronics to kitchen utensils to gold and diamond jewelry. The label, however, may say the product is made elsewhere, because only the raw materials, the basic minerals, came from Africa.

The African continent is rich in natural resources. In northern Africa, drilling and processing petroleum is a major industry, especially in Libya and Algeria. Much of the world's supply of gold and diamonds is mined in southern Africa. Large reserves of copper, oil, tin, manganese, zinc, and cobalt are found in central Africa.

Mining is never a tidy process. In Liberia, rain forest is destroyed to reach the iron ore below. Often, strong chemicals are used, water is contaminated, or large piles of toxic waste are left on the land. The dust kicked up by mining machinery can also pollute the air in the nearby countryside. In the United States, laws require companies to attempt to repair some of the damage by filling in holes, disposing of some toxic waste, and planting trees and other plants on old mining sites. But in Africa, lax environmental laws or lack of enforcement means many mining sites are left as unusable, polluted wastelands. Despite the damage that mining incurs, it is difficult for countries that need money to turn down opportunities for cash. Mount Nimba, for instance, where viviparous toads and many other creatures live, is also a potential source of iron ore.

JUST LISTEN TO THE ELEPHANTS. . .

In 1984 zoologist Katherine Payne was visiting the elephant cage in a zoo when she sensed something strange. She felt vibrations, like the chest-thumping feeling you might experience near a loud bass stereo speaker. Strangely enough, she did not hear anything with her ears. Payne later discovered that elephants can communicate using low frequency pulses humans cannot hear. The pulses travel for miles. It turns out that the elephants all over Africa have been talking to one another over long distances. Yet before Payne's research, scientists had no idea this was occurring. That's amazing, considering that the elephant is one the most studied African animals. Clearly, there is still much to learn about African animals and the continent they inhabit.

4

EASTERN AFRICA: THE GREAT RIFT VALLEY

The continent of Africa is being torn apart. Underneath eastern Africa, tectonic plates are moving away from one another. As the plates move, they rip and tear the African continent above, creating faults, or cracks. Pieces of the continent go in opposite directions and the area in between is stretched thin. This thin area drops, creating valleys, many of which fill with lakes. All this geologic activity has created a dramatic landscape along the Great Rift Valley, a system of tremendous cracks that runs for 3,500 miles (5,600 kilometers) from Djibouti to Malawi. Faults have formed jagged cliffs over which waterfalls tumble. Eruptions of hot magma have created volcanoes such as Mt. Kilimanjaro and Mt. Lengai, which last erupted in 1960.

The Great Rift Valley has two arms, eastern and western. The Eastern Rift runs through Djibouti, Ethiopia, Kenya, and Tanzania, to Malawi. The Western Rift runs along the border between The Democratic Republic of the Congo and Uganda, Rwanda, Burundi, and Tanzania. In Malawi these rifts rejoin. The Great Rift Valley is part of a larger, three-pronged system of rifts that runs north through the Red Sea to Turkey, and eastward through the Gulf of Aden.

In the Great Rift Valley, molten rock called lava flows from inside the earth, filling in some of the faults. As it cools and hardens, the lava forms new tectonic plate material.

This type of geologic activity is usually seen underneath the ocean, in places such as the Mid-Atlantic Ridge, where seafloor spreading is occurring and ocean floor is forming. But scientists can see this happening on dry land in Africa. Tens of millions of years from now, an ocean will occupy Africa's Great Rift Valley, and Somalia may be an island!

The Great Rift Valley was not made by a river but by the earth shifting.
It's still changing as tectonic plates move apart, creating cliffs and volcanoes.
This view of the valley is in Kenya.

LAND OF LAKES

Almost all the large lakes in Africa lie in the Great Rift Valley. The source of the Nile River, Lake Victoria, has the largest surface area of any African lake. Lake Tanganyika, which fills a tremendous geologic fault, is Earth's second-deepest lake, after Russia's Lake Baikal. Eastern Africa's lakes vary from shallow soda lakes hostile to most aquatic life, to clear freshwater lakes that are home to hundreds of fish species.

FLAMINGOS AND LAKES OF SODA

Think first before you swim in an East African lake. Some are soda lakes, with water so corrosive it can blind you and burn off your skin. Soda lakes are salty and alkaline, the opposite of acid. The minerals that make the water alkaline come from the region's volcanic rock.

Not much can live in a soda lake. But algae and bacteria do. In less alkaline lakes, shrimp survive as well. Greater and lesser flamingos eat shrimp, algae, and bacteria by sweeping their bills—upside down—back and forth in the water. A flamingo's bill has a fringe much like a whale's baleen. The flamingo pushes the algae-and-water mixture

Lake Bogonia, in Kenya, lies along the Great Rift Valley. The flamingos get their pink color from shrimp that they eat.

through this fringe to sieve out the edible material. African lakes support millions of flamingos, which look like swirling pink clouds when they rise in large flocks.

THIS PLACE IS REALLY FISHY

Shimmering in the waters of Lake Victoria, Lake Tanganyika, and Lake Malawi are the world's most bizarre fish: cichlids. Cichlids, which can be thumbnail-sized or up to 6 inches (15 centimeters) long, are a family of fish species that evolve quickly, compared to other fish. As a result, hundreds of different cichlid species, each with its own coloration and often strange behaviors, live in these lakes. Lake Malawi has more fish species than the freshwater lakes of Canada, the United States, and Mexico, combined!

THE BIZARRE LIVES OF CICHLID FAMILIES

How cichlids raise their young is definitely strange. In one species, female cichlids live inside abandoned snail shells. A larger male fish protects dozens of these shells as females lay eggs and raise their young. If the male dies for any reason, one of the females in his territory changes into a large male and takes over his job!

Many cichlids are mouth brooders. Eggs are released into the water by the female and fertilized by the male. Then, the female gobbles up the eggs. The eggs hatch inside her mouth! As they grow, the baby fish swim out and feed. But at any sign of danger, they swim back into her mouth and hide.

34

Head rammer cichlids eat the young of mouth brooders. They ram their heads into female cichlids. The startling impact forces the mother to open her mouth, dropping her eggs or hatchlings. The head rammer eats the eggs or young fish! Catfish in the lake take advantage of mouth brooders. When the cichlids are spawning, catfish swim close, eating many of the mouth brooders' eggs. At the same time, the catfish lay their own eggs. The mouth brooder unknowingly gulps up the catfish eggs and raises them as her own!

A cichlid in Lake Tanganyika. Many cichlid species in Africa are in danger because people introduced the Nile perch to their habitat. Nile perch compete for space and often eat cichlids.

CLIMATE OF EASTERN AFRICA

Eastern Africa has a wide variety of climates and biomes. Somalia, which takes up much of a region called the "Horn of Africa," is very dry, with desert and scrubland that support only small bushes and sparse grass. Kenya, just to the south, has grassland and

This black rhinoceros in Amboseli Park, Kenya, has a clear view of Mount Kilimanjaro, but the future for the black rhino is not so clear: It's an endangered species.

35

These elephants are making a meal of acacia bark in Amboseli Park, Kenya.

scrubland, too. Higher areas, such as Kenya's highlands and Ethiopia's uplands, generally receive more rain and are greener and more fertile. Mt. Kenya is surrounded by savanna, yet a hiker climbing up its slopes could walk through jungle, cool montane forest, and then moorland, where giant lobelias and giant heather grow. Finally, a hiker would reach glaciers and snowfields, where the ground is covered by snow year round.

Farther from the Horn of Africa the land receives more rain. Grassland and savanna are common in the lowlands, especially in Tanzania. A much wetter region lies near Lake Victoria, where rain forest and wet montane forest cover both the lowlands and the slopes of volcanic mountains. To the east, wet coastal areas support mangrove swamps.

SCIENCE IN EASTERN AFRICA

Eastern Africa has been the site of many famous scientists' work. In what is now Gombe National Park in Tanzania, Dr. Jane Goodall, a primatologist, studied the behavior of chimpanzees for more than thirty years. On the forested slopes of the Virunga volcanoes, primatologist Dian Fossey observed the family life of mountain gorillas and fought to defeat poachers. In Olduvai Gorge, paleoanthropologists Louis Leakey, Mary Leakey, and their son Richard Leakey found many of the most important fossilized human skulls that have given us clues about our early ancestors. Human footprints they found there are 3.6 million years old! Many other scientific studies continue in eastern Africa. In Kenya's Amboseli National Park, Dr. Cynthia Moss has lived with and studied the family lives of elephants for more than thirty years, identifying each elephant by the shape of its ears! Africa, with its large expanses of land protected in national parks and reserves, is a good site for scientific study.

SPOTLIGHT ON SAVANNA

The savannas, grasslands, and woodlands of eastern Africa support the most spectacular array of ungulates on Earth. Some, such as wildebeests, hartebeests, and hippos, are grazers, meaning they feed on grasses and other nonwoody plants. Giraffes, which can be 18 feet (5.5 meters) tall, dine high in the treetops instead. Giraffes are browsers; they eat pieces of woody plants such as bushes and trees. Their 18-inch (45-centimeter) tongue is prehensile, so it can reach out and pluck even hard-to-reach leaves. Africa's seventy-six species of antelope often browse as well, although they may switch to grazing, according to what food is plentiful.

Elephants and wildebeests may be the most visible grazers, but there are other herbivores at work. Termites eat seeds, grass, trees, and dried manure. The mounds where they live can be 12 feet (3.7 meters) or more tall. In Africa, termites eat a large portion of the plant material. In turn, the termites become food for aardvarks and pangolins, which raid termite nests and lick up the insects with their long tongues. Lions and leopards prey on the aardvarks and pangolins—although getting through a pangolin's tough, overlapping scales can be a challenge.

GREAT CHASES AND GREAT ESCAPES

When antelope and zebras approach a waterhole, they are often wary. They have good reason to be. Lions tend to wait by waterholes until thirst moves herd animals to come for a drink. Then the lions attack. They try to separate a zebra from the herd, then chase it down and kill it. African wild dogs work together, too, in packs of six to ten, to chase down their prey. Sick, injured, and young animals are the most likely to be caught. Cheetahs, the

For every Thompson's gazelle this cheetah catches, there are many more that get away. The cheetah may soon have to defend its meal against lions or hyenas.

37

world's fastest land animals, usually work alone. They can sprint at speeds of up to 70 miles (112 kilometers) per hour when pursuing antelope. But these lean cats tire quickly; often the antelope gets away. Even if a cheetah does capture an animal, it often loses the food to a pack of hyenas, which may chase the cheetah away from a carcass.

ODE TO ELEPHANTS

Never challenge an elephant to a water drinking contest. An African elephant can drink 56 gallons (212 liters) in five minutes. It can slurp up as much as 2.7 gallons with its trunk, then squeeze the water into its mouth. The trunk is also used for many other purposes. An elephant's trunk can smell, grasp branches high on a tree, or even squirt water like a showerhead. Elephants use their trunks to nuzzle family members, too; elephants have a complex social life and strong family ties. African elephants are larger than Asian elephants, a species that lives in India, Sri Lanka, and parts of Southeast Asia.

In 1989, member nations of the Convention on International Trade in Endangered Species of Wild Fauna and Flora (CITES) banned international trade in ivory. The reason for the ban was that elephants were being slaughtered in tremendous numbers for their tusks, which are made of ivory. The ivory was used to make jewelry, furniture, and other items. Following the ban, poaching of elephants decreased 80% because there was very little market for ivory products.

LIVING POOPER-SCOOPERS

With all those giraffes, zebras, antelope, elephants, and other animals on the savanna, you know there must be a lot of animal droppings. The savanna grass might be smothered if it weren't for some living pooper-scoopers: dung beetles. Dung beetles scoop up feces and roll them with their back legs to make balls more than fifteen times their own size. Once the rolling is done, the dung beetles bury the ball and lay an egg on it. When the egg hatches, it is a wiggling, dung-eating larvae, snug in a big ball of food! Eventually it changes into a beetle and crawls out of the ground. Dung beetles help make the soil fertile. Like gardeners adding manure to their gardens, dung beetles help spread fertilizer in the soil. These and other insects as well as microorganisms help dead, decaying material become soil. Fossils prove that dung beetles have been around for seventy-six million years on Earth, and probably even used the rolled dung of dinosaurs to breed.

HIGHS AND LOWS IN EASTERN AFRICA

Mt. Kilimanjaro, a snow-capped volcano, is the highest mountain in Africa, followed by Mt. Kenya. These mountains were built by volcanoes, which spewed out lava, building the mountains higher and higher along Africa's Great Rift Valley. Some volcanoes

The white rhino is light gray. Its name is a mistranslation of the Afrikaans weit, *meaning "wide." This refers to the rhino's mouth, which is broad and flat compared to the black rhino's pointed mouth.*

collapsed, leaving behind craters, tremendous bowl-shaped depressions in the earth. Three such craters are in Kenya's Ngorongoro Conservation Area. The 12-mile (19-kilometer)-wide Ngorongoro crater is the remnant of a volcano that collapsed two million years ago. It is one of the most visited wildlife areas in Africa. The floor of the crater contains grasslands, ponds, marshes, and an incredible number of wild animals, such as buffaloes, zebras, gazelles, elephants, hippos, lions, hyenas, and ostriches.

MARVELOUS MOUNTAIN GORILLAS

Until recently, gorillas were seen as chest-beating, threatening symbols of aggression and violent behavior. Today, scientists know better. Mountain gorillas live peacefully in African rain forests, munching on wild plants. They do not eat other animals. Their lives are relatively quiet, even sluggish. Each family is guarded by a silverback, a large, older male with a silvery back, who will charge anyone who directly threatens the group. But scientists and tourists have been able to sit peacefully nearby as the apes eat, sleep, and play.

Mountain gorillas live in two locales in the mountains on the borders of the Democratic Republic of the Congo, Rwanda, and Uganda. Lowland gorillas, another subspecies, live in low-lying forests nearby and in western Africa. As of 1981, there were only 250 or so mountain gorillas in the Virunga Mountains in the Democratic Republic

This gorilla is quite content to eat foliage in the sunshine. They can be very aggressive when threatened, but won't go out of their way to attack people.

of the Congo and Rwanda, and an equal number in the Bwindi Impenetrable National Park of Uganda. Poaching threatened the survival of the gorillas. Dian Fossey, a woman who studied the apes from 1967 to 1971, fought hard to keep poachers from killing the gorillas. She returned to the Virungas to continue her research, but, sadly, was mysteriously murdered in 1985. Her life is depicted in the film *Gorillas in the Mist*. In the 1980s, conservationists throughout the world worked to educate the public about them. Soon, gorillas were a source of national pride, and the third-largest source of national income, because many tourists came primarily to see the apes. The number of gorillas in the Virungas increased to 320 by 1990.

WARFARE AND WILDLIFE

In many parts of Africa, warfare is endangering people, wildlife, and the general health of the environment. For example, in the 1990s, the threat to mountain gorillas increased dramatically because of conflict between two ethnic groups: the Hutu and Tutsi people of Rwanda. Three-quarters of a million people left Rwanda to escape the violence and settled in and around Virunga National Park. Thousands of needy people pushed into the park and cut down trees to build shelters. Soldiers from both sides roamed the forests. Land mines were placed in parts of the park. Many park staff were killed during the conflict. Today most of the Rwandans have returned to their country. Very few gorillas have been killed so far. But trying to preserve the gorillas and the park where they live is difficult in the midst of political and economic tension. In Rwanda and elsewhere in Africa, warfare threatens people, wildlife, and wild places.

FROM TSETSES TO TOURISTS

Flies may not be your favorite animals, but in a roundabout way, they have been responsible for protecting some of the wild herds in Africa. Tsetse flies, which look like house flies, sometimes inject a dangerous parasite into humans when they bite them. In humans this parasite causes sleeping sickness, a deadly disease if left untreated. Cattle also die from the disease, but native animals such as zebras and giraffes are immune to it. Because of tsetse flies, many people have stayed out of the savannas and miombo woodlands, which harbor infected flies. For this reason the land has not been converted to farms or towns. Large areas of this land have been set aside as wildlife parks. Tourists who visit these areas ride in air-conditioned, closed vehicles. Since they are not in the areas very long, they do not have much risk of being bitten by the flies. The tourist trade, and the money it brings in, gives people an additional reason to protect the land and the wildlife that live on it. Yet not everyone is pleased about African wildlife parks. Some native people who lived on these lands before the parks were established want better access to the parks, because they are traditional hunting grounds and the source of their livelihoods.

5

SOUTHERN AFRICA

Lying on the western edge of southern Africa is one of Earth's strangest deserts: the Namib. In the Namib, spiders do cartwheels and blind moles swim through sand. Plants can live two thousand years. Geckos chirp all night, like noisy crickets. Diamonds lie under the sand.

The Namib is only one of southern Africa's many regions famous for fabulous scenery and remarkable wildlife. Southern Africa is also the site of the spectacular Victoria Falls, the Okavango Delta, the Kalahari Desert, and the Etosha Pan.

THE BIG BOWL

Southern Africa begins at the southern end of the Great Rift Valley near Lake Malawi. It encompasses the countries of Botswana, Lesotho, Malawi, Mozambique, Namibia, South Africa, Swaziland, and Zimbabwe, along with the large island of Madagascar. Some geographers also include the mainland countries of Angola and Zambia.

Southern Africa is made up almost entirely of a tremendous plateau—a raised area of land. The plateau has raised edges that form a shallow bowl that tilts slightly toward the Drakensberg Mountains in the southeast. Outside of the plateau, a low-lying coastal plain forms the country of Mozambique.

Southern Africa supports a variety of biomes. In the north and east are savannas and grasslands, like those in eastern Africa. The Namib Desert borders the southwest coast. Inland is the Kalahari Desert, which combines both semidesert and steppe. Along the extreme southern coast is a cooler, wetter region with evergreen trees and shrubs. The Drakensberg Mountains also support a number of different habitats because of variations in altitude.

MARVELOUS MADAGASCAR

Where do chameleons climb and lemurs leap? On the island of Madagascar. The fourth-largest island in the world, Madagascar is located 250 miles (403 kilometers) off the southeast coast of Africa. It has many different habitats: deserts, rain forests, grasslands, mountains, and mangrove swamps. Madagascar is famous for its biological diversity. Three-quarters of the island's 200,000 plant and animal species are endemic, meaning they live nowhere else in the world! Geologists think that Madagascar was connected to Africa about sixty-five million years ago, but then broke away. Since then, Madagascar's animals have evolved in relative isolation, becoming very different from the ones on mainland Africa.

Lemurs, Madagascar's most famous animal, are small, furry primates that seem more like cats than apes or monkeys. They range from the 1-ounce (30-gram) mouse lemur to the 15-pound (7-kilogram) indri. Ring-tailed lemurs and white-ruffed lemurs are common in American zoos. Lemurs eat bamboo, fruit, tree leaves, insects, resin, and other foods.

Madagascar's biodiversity is in danger because people cut down trees to clear the land for growing crops and cattle grazing. Logs are also used for fuel wood, building material, and for export to make furniture. Most of Madagascar's forests have been destroyed. Parks and nature preserves help protect some of the remnants. Many conservationists in Madagascar and worldwide hope that ecotourism—people visiting parks to see their unique wildlife and plants—will enable native Malagasies to make a living from forests without destroying them. Scientists and conservationists in Madagascar are working with the people who live near parks to improve farming and forestry techniques. In this way, they can produce more crops and lumber on smaller areas of land, and reduce erosion.

NAMIB DESERT: SAND, SKELETONS, AND DIAMONDS

In the language of the Nama people who live in the desert, Namib means "area of nothingness." The Namib is so dry that parts of the desert may go for several years without rain. Nevertheless, this desert is home to large mammals such as the elephant, antelope, and baboon, and it supports more animal species than any other dune area on Earth. Forty-five lizard species alone live in the Namib.

*Namib Desert, in Namibia, has the highest sand dunes in the world.
Desert terrain can be quite varied, as you can see from the photo at right.*

The Namib is a coastal desert. It stretches 1,200 miles (1,935 kilometers) from Angola to South Africa, in a strip 50 to 100 miles (80 to 160 kilometers) wide. Sediment carried by the Orange River out of South Africa to the coast formed the Namib's sandy expanses. These sediments also brought diamonds to the Namib, giving the region the name "Diamond Coast." Mining operations in the Namib sometimes sift $1 million worth of diamonds out of the sand and gravel in a day!

Diamond Coast is not the only nickname for the Namib. It is also called the "skeleton coast." Offshore winds and fog make sea travel perilous. Wrecked ships and the bodies of sailors and whales and other sea animals are blown inland to the beaches. Dry air and blowing sand scour the bleached white bones, leaving them exposed.

PRECIOUS WATER

Not all of the Namib is dunes. North of the Kuiseb River, which cuts the Namib in two, are gravel plains where elephants, zebras, giraffes, and antelope live. The Kuiseb River itself may only fill with water about once a year. Antelope and elephants walk dozens of miles to drink from its waters. As the river dries out, it forms small water holes

44

Desert elephants in the Namib Desert must walk miles for water.
They play an important part in maintaining water holes year-round.

where birds gather. Sand grouse soak their breast feathers in the water and fly back to their nests where their chicks sip from the wet feathers. Sand grouse may fly as far as 100 miles (160 kilometers) round trip just to reach a water hole and return home! Even after water holes have dried up, water remains under the riverbed. Trees and shrubs with deep roots tap this resource. Baboons dig and expand water holes to get to the underground water.

LAND OF THE FOG DRINKERS

Like the Atacama Desert in Chile, South America, the Namib Desert receives moisture from fog. For about sixty days per year, warm air from the Atlantic Ocean blows over cold Antarctic water just offshore. The moist, warm air cools as it passes over the cold current and the water condenses, forming fog. The fog is blown inland as much as 30 miles (48 kilometers).

Because rain is scarce, many animals have adapted to take advantage of this fog. Black beetles climb to the tops of dune ridges and face the incoming fog, their backs tilted up. The fog collects on their backs and rolls down into their mouths. Snakes and geckos lick the fog that collects on their bodies. Other animals such as giraffes get water from what they eat: the leaves of acacia trees or the pulpy fruits of naras plants.

Plants gather water in a variety of ways. The *Welwitschia mirabilis*, one of Earth's oldest plant species, has deep tap roots, plus shallow lateral roots that spread out under the sand. It can also absorb water from fog through its leathery leaves. A welwitschia plant only has two of these leaves that split, fray, and curl during its lifetime—which may be two thousand years!

WHEN THE RAIN COMES

When rain does arrive in the Namib, the gravel plains turn green with grass. Bushes grow fresh leaves. Insects called blue weevils emerge. Most of the time they live as eggs or larvae in the ground, but after it rains, blue weevils hatch, mate, lay eggs, and die, all in just a few weeks. Toad grasshoppers, colored like sand, also emerge after rain. Birds such as finch larks feast on the weevils. After the rain-watered plants have produced seeds and dried up in the desert sun, they crumble and blow around in the wind. Small insects that live in the sand dunes rely on these tidbits of food to survive.

SURPRISES AND SURVIVORS IN SAND

The dunes of the Namib are full of animals with surprising adaptations. When threatened by a predator, the golden wheel spider curls up its legs and rolls down the dunes like a wheel to get away. Sidewinding adders are snakes that have eyes on top of their heads. They bury their bodies in the sand, but with their uncovered eyes can keep watch for passing lizards to eat! Legless lizards slither through the sand, smelling and pursuing insects. Golden moles tunnel through sand, breathing the air trapped between sand grains. This blind animal hunts spiders, beetles, and legless lizards by sensing smells and detecting the vibrations of moving creatures.

OUCH, THAT'S HOT!

Sand dunes can be difficult to walk on. The sand shifts underfoot, and the surface can be a sizzling 170°F (77°C). To keep from burning its feet, one lizard species in the Namib alternately lifts its feet to let them cool off! Sidewinding adders, like the sidewinding rattlesnakes of North America, travel by pushing their bodies in a looping pattern. This helps them move quickly and get a grip on the sand.

Desert chameleons are natural solar collectors. These lizards change color to regulate their body temperature. In the morning, after the long cold night, they turn black, which helps them absorb heat. In the afternoon, they turn a lighter color, which absorbs less heat, so they remain cool. Many other animals just stay buried during the hottest parts of the day, then emerge at night.

Traveling inland from the Namib, you'll encounter the Okavango Delta. The Okavango Delta is a wetland bigger than Massachusetts. This mosaic of islands, soggy soil, and interlaced, slow-moving streams is full of fish, birds, crocodiles, lions, and other wildlife. Unlike most deltas, the Okavango is an inland delta. It formed when the land shifted, blocking a river's flow.

The Okavango's water comes from rain that falls in the mountains of Angola and travels down the Okavango River flooding the delta each March or April. Local rainfall adds water to the delta. The Okavango has incredibly clean fresh water, which is naturally filtered as it flows among the plants and through the sand. This water flows slowly through the delta, almost 95 percent of it evaporating along the way. For the Okavango Delta to remain wet, it must receive regular floods. During seven years of drought in the 1980s, flooding did not occur. As a result, many plants died and large numbers of animals starved.

Amphibious Antelope and other Animals

Antelope, like deer, usually live on dry ground. But in the Okavango, a type of antelope called sitatunga spends time underwater. Sitatungas dive and feed on underwater plants. If pursued, they hide in the water among reeds, and submerge themselves, with only their nostrils showing!

The Okavango supports a large number of antelope species, such as reedbucks, impalas, greater kudus, common waterbucks, lechwes, tsessebes, sable antelope, and roan antelope. It also has the wildebeest, a large antelope that looks more like a cow and weighs up to 600 pounds (272 kilograms.)

Wildlife is abundant in the Okavango. Large wading birds, such as wattled cranes, egrets, storks, pelicans, and ibis, hunt fish and frogs in the deeper water. Butterflies drink at pud-

Sitatungas spend a great deal of time in water

dles. Fish eagles, which resemble the bald eagles of North America, dive into the Okavango to catch fish. Hippos munch on underwater plants. Water lilies and papyrus—the same reeds that the ancient Egyptians used to make paper—grow in the wettest areas, providing good hiding places not only for sitatungas but also for waterbirds. Islands that have formed when muck settled around termite mounds provide places for birds to raise their young. Thousands of zebras, elephants, buffalo, and antelope also drink the Okavango's water, then move out into nearby savannas, acacia woodlands, and mopani woodlands to feed. Riding along with them are helpful hitchhikers: oxpeckers, birds that perch on the backs of herd animals and eat ticks, flies, and other bloodsucking parasites.

FENCES AND FAILURES

Until this century, not many people went into the Okavango because it was home to large numbers of tsetse flies. But in the 1960s, 1970s, and 1980s, the government undertook a massive effort to exterminate the flies by spraying pesticides on wet places where the flies lived. Soon after the tsetse flies were exterminated, people and their cattle moved into the Okavango Delta and nearby grasslands.

Cattle farmers probably would have moved farther into the delta, were it not for another disease. Some wild buffalo carry hoof-and-mouth disease, which can kill cattle. In 1982 a 150-mile (242-kilometer) fence, the Buffalo Fence, was built to separate the wild buffalo of the Okavango from the cattle that grazed outside the area. On the positive side, this fence, and similar ones in Botswana, have kept cattle out of parks, leaving more room for wildlife. Hoof-and-mouth disease has not been much of a problem. But the fences interfere with the natural movement of herd animals such as wildebeest. These animals migrate, move from place to place, to reach new grazing grounds and water. During droughts, tens of thousands of wildebeest have died, their carcasses piling up along the fences they could not cross.

THE KALAHARI

Like the Okavango, the Kalahari is full of wildlife. Twenty-two species of antelope roam the region. Lions and leopards hunt, cheetahs sprint, and wild dogs team up to bring down prey. Antbears and aardwolves paw their way into termite mounds and lick up termites. Ostriches, the largest birds on Earth, incubate their eggs. Families of meerkats live in colonies like prairie dogs, keeping a lookout for predators.

Twice as big as Arizona, the Kalahari Desert is located in Botswana, South Africa, and Namibia. Sections of the Kalahari are partly protected in the Central Kalahari Game Preserve and the Kalahari Gemsbok National Park. Lying on a plateau 3,200 feet (1,000 meters) high, the Kalahari is blanketed by sand as deep as 300 feet (90 meters). Parts of the desert have rocky outcrops and sand dunes. Although commonly called a desert, the Kalahari receives 5 to 25 inches (46 to 64 centimeters) of rain, making it mostly a semi-desert, instead. The climate is generally dry, hot, and sometimes windy. Air temperatures can reach 120°F (49°C) in the heat of summer.

OUT OF THE FIRE AND INTO THE PAN

The Kalahari is dotted with a thousand or so pans, shallow depressions that fill up with water after heavy rains, when rivers flow. The pans provide a place for zebras, wildebeest, gazelles, and lions to bathe and drink. Some large pans are like lakes, as much as 3 miles (4.8 kilometers) across. When the water evaporates, a crust of salt is left behind. Wild zebras and wildebeest lick the salt, the way domesticated horses and cows lick blocks of salt. The salt contains minerals important to the animals' health.

Surrounding the pans is savanna, where grass, bushes, and occasional trees grow. Acacias, with their long thorns and narrow fernlike leaves, grow as shrubs on much of the land. (Many acacia species grow to tree size in other African savannas.) Camel thorn, shepherd's tree, and gemsbok bean are other common Kalahari plants.

BOUNTIFUL BAOBAB

Growing on Africa's savannas and in the Kalahari are huge, thick-trunked trees that can live more than a thousand years. These trees, called baobabs, have twisted branches that resemble roots, making them look like they are growing upside down. A baobab tree begins growing as a straight, upright tree. But as it grows older, it twists and thickens. Eventually, a baobab's trunk can be 30 feet (9 meters) in diameter and 60 feet (18 meters) high. The trees only grow leaves after it rains.

Many animals depend on baobabs. Yellow-collared lovebirds, lilac-breasted rollers, yellow-billed hornbills, and red-headed weaverbirds nest in baobabs. Male weaverbirds make nests from grass and suspend them from baobab branches. The female weaverbird goes on a tour, examining the nests before moving in with the male who has built the best one.

Bush babies, small, long-tailed primates, make their homes in holes in baobabs. Both bush babies and bats drink the nectar of the baobab's large white flowers. When the tree forms fruit, baboons gather it and feed on the sweet, seedy pulp. Beetles, mealybugs, caterpillars, and other insects also live in the tree and eat its leaves and wood, too. Elephants strip away and eat baobab bark. Fortunately, the trees can regrow some bark to cover the holes left by the elephants.

THE HORNBILL'S HIDEOUT

Have you ever cooked breakfast with a hornbill perched on your head? Scientist Delia Owens has, as she describes in the book *Cry of the Kalahari*, which she wrote with her

husband Mark. Mark and Delia Owens are scientists who studied lions and brown hyenas in the Kalahari Desert. They also became familiar with other animals, such as hornbills, large-billed birds that stole food from their campsite on a regular basis.

Their fellow campers, yellow-billed hornbills, have unusual nesting habits. The female moves into a hollow in a baobab tree and seals herself inside, closing the opening with mud and feces, leaving a small slit, like a window. Through this slit, the male passes fruit, insects, seeds, and other food to the female. She stays inside for six weeks, laying eggs, incubating them, and then keeping the young chicks warm. The wall keeps the eggs and hatchlings safe from animals that otherwise might eat them. The male is busy, flying to and fro with food for the female and hatchlings. When the young hornbills are large enough, the female breaks out of the nest, then rebuilds the wall, so her brood is safe inside. Then both she and the male feed the young together, through a small slit. After three more weeks, the young break out of their walled home and take their first flights.

ETOSHA'S CYCLE OF LIFE

Northwest of the Kalahari Desert is the Etosha Pan, a place where salt-crusted land sparkles in the sun. One of the largest regions of salt flats on Earth, the Etosha Pan stretches over 1,800 square miles (4,662 square kilometers). These salt flats are the remnants of dried-up lakes and rivers. When the water evaporates, it leaves salt behind on the surface of the ground. Most of this region, rich in wildlife, is preserved in Etosha National Park.

The Etosha region, like other grasslands and savannas in Africa, has a distinctive seasonal cycle of life. Most of the year, Etosha is dry. In late January, the land is dusty and the air is hot. Then, thunderclouds form and heavy rains fall for several months, drenching the parched ground and filling the Etosha Pan with water. A tremendous lake forms, 50 miles (80 kilometers) wide yet hardly more than knee deep, providing water for animals such as zebras, gazelles, and many birds.

As water becomes scarce during the dry season in Etosha National Park, in Namibia, animals gather for a drink. Predators move in looking for vulnerable prey.

WILD WET SEASON

In the wet season, catfish that have hidden underground in moist mud during the dry season emerge and lay eggs. Suddenly, the lake is filled with fish. Giant bullfrogs lay eggs. Long-legged waterbirds such as ibises and storks flock to the lake to feed on the fish. Grass and puffy red wildflowers and tiny yellow wildflowers sprout and grow on the surrounding grasslands. Doves, ground squirrels, wildebeest, antelope, and many other animals raise young at this time of year, when food is plentiful. Cheetahs chase down young zebras to feed to their kittens. Bat-eared foxes, with their tremendous ears, listen for insects crawling underground, then quickly dig them up to feed themselves and their young.

SHRINKING WATER SOURCES

After three more months, the lake begins drying up. The catfish are crowded in the shrinking lake, where pelicans, yellow-billed storks, and ibises feast on the easily caught fish. Fortunately, water holes, fed by underground water, still remain along the edges of the lake. More and more zebras, giraffes, wildebeest, antelope, and the lions that hunt them, gather there. Elephants wander in, too. The grass that grew after the rains matures and dries out, so wildebeest and zebras travel hundreds of miles in search of better grazing areas.

THE TIME OF THIRST

After September, the water holes shrink, and the weather becomes hotter and drier. The mud of the lake bed cracks and dries in the sun. Light rains bring only some relief. Wildebeest and zebra move back toward the Etosha grasslands, in anticipation of the rain. Catfish and frogs again dig deep underground. Life is on hold, waiting for the heavy rains. Then, in January, the rain returns, and the cycle begins again.

The animals of the Namib need fog, the creatures of the Okavango need river water, and the animals of the Etosha need the yearly rains. Each year, the search for water and seasonal cycles of wet and dry control the lives of animals and plants throughout Africa.

CONCLUSION

LOOKING TO THE FUTURE

Africa is a continent rich in natural resources, from mineral wealth to amazing wildlife herds. But Africa's human population, the fastest growing on Earth, is taking a heavy toll on the land. Good land for growing crops and grazing cattle has become scarce. Water for drinking and nurturing crops is often hard to find. Wildlife and natural environments are being wiped out as desperate people hunt for meat and fuel wood.

Many African countries are torn by unstable governments, wars, ethnic violence, and political turmoil. Tens of millions of Africans live as refugees, forced out of their own countries by violence, drought, or disease. Many countries with stable governments and strong environmental laws are now challenged because of an influx of large numbers of refugees. Large international corporations have taken advantage of lax environmental laws and weak economies by moving in to reap the profits from minerals and other natural resources.

Despite these extremely difficult conditions, some international organizations, African nations, and concerned citizens are trying to conserve wildlife, protect the soil, and create a healthy environment for the people of Africa.

In western Africa, for example, United States Peace Corps volunteers are showing native people how to modify their cooking stoves to make them more efficient, so they burn less wood. This will help conserve the remaining trees. In 1998 the United Nations passed the Convention to Combat Desertification, which will fund programs to help people conserve fragile soils and trees.

South Africa's government, specifically its Natal Parks Board, has helped reintroduce

This rhino has been killed for its horn. Poaching—the illegal killing of wildlife—is endangering many animals such as rhinos.

zebras, giraffes, white rhinos, and black rhinos to areas where they had been exterminated. Zimbabwe has managed parks so successfully that some have too many elephants and must move them to other areas.

In southern Africa, thousands of private ranches are providing habitat for wild animals such as antelope, elephants, lions, leopards, rhinos, and zebras. Hunters come from all over the world to visit these farms and hunt. In contrast, not everyone agrees with the killing of wildlife for meat and hides or for sport. But even these programs give people a variety of ways to make money off wildlife, and provide an alternative to illegally destroying the wild populations of Africa's parks and preserves.

In some countries, Africans are risking their lives to save the environment. Nigerian writer Ken Saro-Wiwa organized protests against the pollution caused by oil drilling in the Niger River Delta. Winner of the international Goldman Environmental Prize, Saro-Wiwa was jailed and hanged on charges that were called "politically motivated" by the human rights group Amnesty International. In Kenya, Dr. Wangari Maathai has spent decades helping to establish a grassroots movement to plant trees to replace those that were destroyed. But her activism has, at times, put her life in danger because of the shifting political scene.

From park rangers fighting poachers to citizens protesting pollution to schoolteachers educating children about wildlife, many people are working not only to protect wildlife but also to ensure a healthy environment for future generations of Africans.

GLOSSARY

biodiversity—the variety of species of plants and animals in a given area

biome—an area that has a certain kind of climate and a certain kind of community of animals and plants

climate—a region's long-term weather conditions

deforestation—the destruction of forest by cutting, burning, or other means

delta—the mud, sand, and other material deposited at the mouth of a river where the water slows down

desert—a biome that occurs where precipitation is less than 10 inches (25 centimeters) per year

desertification—the degradation of dry lands that leaves the soil infertile, barren, and vulnerable to erosion

erosion—the wearing away of rocks and soil by wind, water, or other forces

fallow period—the time when a farmer does not grow crops on the land in order to allow the soil to become fertile again

famine—an extreme shortage of food

fault—a fracture in Earth's surface

grazer—an animal that feeds on plants, such as grasses, that are not woody. (Bushes and trees, which are woody, are eaten by plant-eaters called browsers.)

Great Rift Valley—a geological system of faults running from the Red Sea to Mozambique

Pangaea—the original landmass that existed 250 million years ago, when the separate continents we know today were all joined together

Panthalassa—the ocean that surrounded Pangaea

plateau—a large, relatively flat area of land raised above surrounding land

poaching—illegal hunting or fishing

Sahara—the world's largest desert region, covering most of northern Africa

Sahel—a semiarid region south of the Sahara, covering portions of Senegal, Mauritania, Mali, Burkina Faso, Ghana, Niger, Nigeria, Chad, Cameroon, and the Central African Republic

savanna—a type of grassland that has widely scattered trees

sediment—particles that are transported and deposited by wind, water, or ice

soda lake—an alkaline lake containing large amounts of carbonates

steppe—a dry, treeless grassland

tectonic plate—a large piece of Earth's crust that slides over the molten rock below it, gradually shifting its position on Earth's surface

transpiration—loss of water through the surfaces of a plant

tropical rain forest—a forest biome found in the tropics and characterized by warmth, very heavy rainfall and high species diversity

ungulate—a hoofed mammal

woodland—a region that has trees, spread apart, not as close together as those of a forest. A forest has trees that are close enough together to form a continuous canopy.

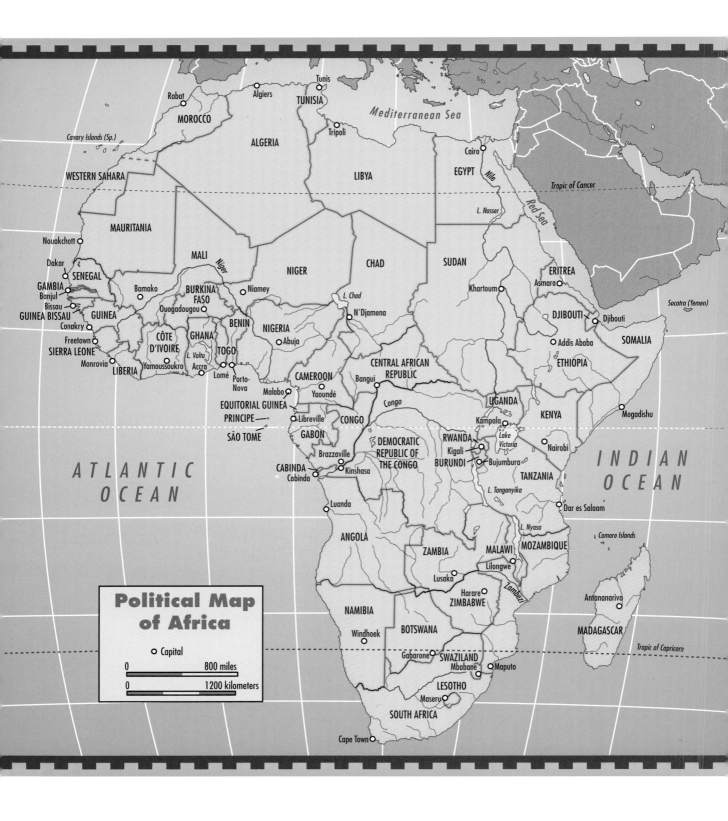

Political Map of Africa

o Capital

0 — 800 miles
0 — 1200 kilometers

INDEPENDENT COUNTRIES OF AFRICA AND THEIR CAPITAL CITIES

NAME	CAPITAL
Algeria	Algiers
Angola	Luanda
Benin	Port-Novo
Botswana	Gabarone
Burkina Faso	Ouagadougou
Burundi	Bujumbura
Cameroon	Yaoundé
Cape Verde	Praia
Central African Republic	Bangui
Chad	N'Djamena
Comoros	Moroni
Congo	Brazzaville
Côte d'Ivoire	Abidjan
Democratic Republic of the Congo	Kinshasa
Djibouti	Djibouti
Equatorial Guinea	Malabo
Eritrea	Asmara
Ethiopia	Addis Ababa
Gabon	Libreville
Gambia	Banjul
Ghana	Accra
Guinea	Conakry
Guinea-Bissau	Bissau
Kenya	Nairobi
Lesotho	Maseru
Liberia	Monrovia
Libya	Tripoli
Madagascar	Antananarivo
Malawi	Lilongwe
Mali	Bamako
Mauritania	Nouakchott
Mauritius	Port Louis
Morocco	Rabat

Name	Capital
Mozambique	Maputo
Namibia	Windhoek
Niger	Niamey
Nigeria	Abuja
Rwanda	Kigali
São Tomé and Príncipe	São Tomé
Senegal	Dakar
Seychelles	Victoria
Sierra Leone	Freetown
Somalia	Mogadishu
South Africa	Cape Town, Pretoria, Bloemfontein
Sudan	Khartoum
Swaziland	Mbabane
Tanzania	Dar es Salaam
Togo	Lomé
Tunisia	Tunis
Uganda	Kampala
Zambia	Lusaka
Zimbabwe	Harare

INDEPENDENT COUNTRY LOCATED PARTLY IN AFRICA, PARTLY IN ASIA

Name	Capital
Egypt	Cairo

DEPENDENCIES IN AFRICA

Name	Capital
Canary Islands	Santa Cruz de Tenerife
Madeira Islands	Funchal
Réunion	Saint-Denis
St. Helena Island Group	Jamestown
Western Sahara	Aaiun

(Rodrigues, also Rodriguez, is a dependency of Mauritius)

FURTHER READING

BOOKS

(Books for young readers are marked with an asterisk.)

Alden, Peter C. *National Audubon Society Field Guide to African Wildlife*. New York: Alfred A. Knopf, 1995.

Arritt, Susan. *The Living Earth Book of Deserts*. Pleasantville, NY: Reader's Digest, 1993.

* Bash, Barbara. *Tree of Life: The World of the African Baobab*. San Francisco: Sierra Club Books, 1989.

* Brandenburg, Jim. *Sand and Fog: Adventures in South Africa*. New York: Walker and Company, 1994.

* Brill, Marlene Targ. *Libya*. Enchantment of the World series. Chicago: Children's Press, 1987.

* Colin, Sale, editor. *The Reader's Digest Children's Atlas of the World*. Westport, CT: Reader's Digest, 1998.

Elphick, Jonathan, general editor. *The Atlas of Bird Migration*. New York: Random House, 1995.

* Kapit, Wynn. *The Geography Coloring Book*. New York: HarperCollins, revised edition, 1998.

* Kreikemeier, Gregory Scott. *Come with Me to Africa: A Photographic Journey*. New York: Golden Books, 1993.

Owens, Delia, and Mark Owens. *Cry of the Kalahari*. New York: Houghton Mifflin Company, 1984.

McClung, Robert M. *Last of the Wild: Vanished and Vanishing Giants of the Animal World*. New Haven, CT: Linnet Books, 1997.

* Simon, Scoones. *The Sahara and Its People*. New York: Thomson Learning, 1993.

Smith, Anthony. *The Great Rift: Africa's Changing Valley*. New York: Sterling Publishing, 1988.

SELECTED ARTICLES ABOUT AFRICA

Bass, Thomas A. "This African Lake Turns Out to Be a Fine Kettle of Fish," *Smithsonian*, December, 1988, 145-154.

Caputo, Robert. "Lifeline for a Nation—Zaire River." *National Geographic*, July 1995, 3-35.

Chadwick, Doug. "Ndoki—Last Place on Earth," *National Geographic*, July 1995, 2-45.

Chadwick, Doug. "A Place for Parks in the New South Africa," *National Geographic*, July 1996, 2-41.

Lee, Douglas B. "Oakavango Delta: Old Africa's Last Refuge," *National Geographic*, December 1990, 39-69.

McRae, Michael. "Road Kill in Cameroon," *Natural History*, February 1997, 36-47, 74.

Owens, Mark and Delia. "Two Against the Odds: Our Fight to Save Zambia's Elephants," *International Wildlife*, September-October, 1992, 4-13.

Schaller, George B., and Salopek, Paul F. "The Mountain Gorillas of Africa," *National Geographic*, October 1995, 58-83.

Stager, Curt. "Africa's Great Rift," *National Geographic*, May 1990, 2-51.

Swerdlow, Joel L., Michael Parfit, Erla Zwingle, and T. R. Reid, "Population," "Human Migration," Women and Population," "Feeding the Planet," in a special population issue, *National Geographic*, October 1988, 2-75.

Theroux, Peter, "The Imperiled Nile Delta," *National Geographic*, January 1997, 2-35.

WORLD WIDE WEB

Web sites come and go very quickly, so it is best to use a search program to search for key words and phrases such as Africa, African wildlife, Kalahari, Sahara, and so on. Below is one site where you might want to begin your search:

African Wildlife Foundation
http://www.awf.org
Articles and photos about conservation of wildlife in Africa. Connections to other sites.

INDEX

Page numbers in *boldface italics* refer to illustrations.

Algeria, 13, *24*
Amboseli Park, *35*, *36*
Angola, 13, 42, 47
animals, 9, 18, 19, 26–30, 36–41, 43–51, 54
Antarctica, 5, 7
aquifers, 17
Asia, 5, 7
aspergillis, 23
Aswan High Dam, 18
Atlantic Ocean, 10, *20*
Atlas Mountains, 10, 14, 19
Australia, 5, 7

baobabs, 49
basins, 10
Benin, 13, 30
biodiversity, 43
biomes, 35–36, 42
birds, 19, 21, 26, 29, 30, 33–34, 45–51
Botswana, 13, 42, 49
browsers, 37
Burkina Faso, 13, 30
Burundi, 13, 32
bushmeat, 28, 29

Cameroon, 13
Central Africa, 13, 25–29
Central African Republic, 13, 25
Chad, 13
chotts, 17
climate, 11, 14, 15, 19, 23, 35–36, 49
continents, 5, 7
Convention to Combat Desertification, 23, 53
coral reefs, 23–24
Côte d'Ivoire, 13, 30, *30*, 31
craters, 39

dates, 18
deforestation, 29, 30
dehydration, 15

Democratic Republic of Congo, 9, 10, 13, 25, *27*, 32, 39
desertification, 21, 22, *24*
deserts, 10, 11, 14–18, 23–24, 42–46
Djibouti, 13, 21, 32
Drakensberg Mountains, 10, 42, 43
droughts, 21, 23

earthquakes, 5, 11
Eastern Africa, 13, 32–41
Efé people, 28, *28*
Egypt, 11, 13, 18–19, 21
elephants, 27–28, 31, 38, *45*
Equatorial Guinea, 13
ergs, 17
erosion, 43
Ethiopia, 13, 32, 36
Etosha National Park, *51*
Etosha Pan, 42, 50–52
Europe, 5, 7

fallow period, 21
famine, 23
faults, 32
fences, 48
fish, 34–35, 50
flamingos, 33–34, *34*
Fossey, Dian, 36, 40
fossils, 11, 36

Gabon, 13, 25
Gambia, 13, 30
Ghana, 13, 30
glaciation, 11
Goodall, Jane, 36
gorillas, 36, 39–41, *40*
grazers, 37
Great Rift Valley, 10, 11, 32–41, *33*, *34*
Guinea, 13, 29
Guinea-Bisseau, 13

hammadas, 17

herbivores, 27
hornbills, 50, *50*

Indian Ocean, 10
insects, 28, 38, 46
irrigation, 23
ivory, 38

Kalahari Desert, 10, 42, 48–50
Kenya, *8*, 13, 32, *33*, 35–36, *35*, *36*, 39, 54–55
Kuiseb River, 44

Lake Assal, 11
Lake Bogonia, *34*
Lake Malawi, 34, 42
lakes, 11, 33–34
Lake Tanganyika, 11, 33, 34, *35*
Lake Victoria, 11, 18, 33, 34
lava, 32, 38
lemurs, 43
Lese people, 28
Lesotho, 13, 42
Liberia, 13
Libya, 13, *15*
logging, 29, 30

Madagasgar, 13, 25, 43
Malawi, 13, 32, 42
Mali, 13, *16*
Mauritania, 13, 21
Mauritius, 25
Mediterranean Sea, 10, 19
mining, 31, 44, 53
Morocco, 13, 19, *20*, 21
Moss, Cynthia, 36
mountains, 5, 10, 17, 38
Mount Kilimanjaro, 11, 32, *35*, 38
Mount Lengai, 32
Mount Nimba, 31
Mozambique, 13, 42

Namib Desert, 10, 42–46, *44*, *45*

Namibia, 13, 42, *44*, 49, *51*
Niger, 13, 30
Nigeria, 13, 30, 54
Nile River, 11, 18–19, 21, 33
Nile Valley, 14
North America, 5, 7
Northern Africa, 10, 13, 14–24

oases, 17
okapis, 27, *27*
Okavango Delta, 42, 47–48
Olduvai Gorge, 11, 36

Pangaea, 5
Panthalassa, 5
pet trade, 29
plants, 15, 46–48
plateaus, 10, 42
population, 11

rainfall, 15, 17, 29, 45–46, 49
rain forests, 9, 10, 15, 24–28, 36
Red Sea, 10

regs, 17
Réunion, 25
rivers, 11, 18–19, 21, 33, 44
Rodriguez, 25
Rwanda, 13, 25, 32, 39–41
Sahara Desert, 10, 11, 14–18, 23–24
Sahel, 21, 23, 29
sandstorms, 16
savannas, 9, 29, 36–37, 42, 49
scientific study, 36, 50
sediment, 18
Senegal, 13
Seychelles, 25
Sierra Leone, 13
sitatungas, 47, *47*
soda lakes, 33
Somalia, 13, 35
South Africa, 13, 42, 44, 49, 53–54
South America, 5, 7
Southern Africa, 13, 42–52
steppes, 10
Sudan, 13

Swaziland, 13, 42

Tai National Park, 30, *30*
Tadrart Mountains, *15*
Tanzania, 13, 32, 36
tectonic plates, 5, 32
Togo, 13
tsetse flies, 41, 48
Tuareg, *16*
Tunisia, 13, 21

Uganda, 13, 25, 32, 39, 40
ungulates, 27, 36–37

Victoria Falls, 42
volcanoes, 5, 11, 38

warfare, 40–41, 53
Western Africa, 13, 29–31
Western Sahara, 13
woodlands, 9, 21

Zambia, 13, 42
Zimbabwe, 13, 42, 54